ANDREA HANEY POOLE

The Long Way I Came

Contents

Acknowledgments

This book exists because of love, resilience, and the people who never stopped believing in me—even as I still learn to believe in myself.

To my husband, Michael— my greatest encourager, my calm in every storm, my Bear. You have walked beside me through every chapter of my life, including the hardest ones to write. Thank you for holding space for my grief, for making me laugh when everything felt heavy, and for building a life with me that feels like safety in its purest form. Our home, our peace, our little rituals—they exist because of the way you love.

To my mother, my Marmie— your courage has always been my compass. Long before I had the words to understand it, you were teaching me strength wrapped in softness. You rebuilt your life with grace and stubborn hope, and watching you rise helped me learn how to rise myself. You are the reason I am free.

To my brother, Bubs— brilliant, loyal, hilarious, and deeply kind. You have always seen the world through a lens uniquely your own, and you let me into that view with a generosity I've never taken for granted. You taught me how to protect someone I love, how to find joy in the smallest moments, and how connection can transcend the hardest seasons.

To the grandparents whose love shaped our lives— your lives remain stitched into every chapter of mine, and I think of you often. From patience learned in weekend visits to the tenderness in caring for you as the years unfolded, your influence shaped the foundation I stand on. Thank you for the stories, the steadiness, and the lessons I carry forward with gratitude.

And to Kitty, Nicky, Schmidt, Cici, Jess, and Bootsie— my constant companions and teachers of tenderness. You have each been a reminder that love can appear in many forms and often arrives exactly when we need it most.

Kitty and Nicky, your spirits live on in the joy and softness of the ones who came after, and I carry you with me always.

To Allan — thank you for seeing my potential before I fully stepped into it. Your belief in authenticity, steady kindness, and willingness to challenge me to stop limiting myself have helped shape this book. I'm grateful for the impact you've had on my work and growth.

And finally, to every reader who has walked through pain and kept going — this book is for you. May you always find your spark, your courage, and your own long way home to yourself.

I

Part One

Before I knew how to name myself, I learned how to read the room.
This was the season of early knowing—of sensing what was expected, what was safe, and what needed to stay hidden. Long before I understood choice or agency, I was absorbing the world as it was handed to me. These pages return to the places where my story began, where the foundations were laid—uneven, imperfect, but formative all the same.

1

The Long Way Begins

I was never meant to stay in my small hometown in Tennessee. I knew it the way you know when a storm is coming—a stirring, the smell of change, something electric in the air, something restless in me. While others settled into the rhythm of small-town life, I dreamed beyond the city limits, losing myself in stories that promised there was more waiting for me somewhere out there. Even then, I knew I was different. Not better—just restless. I didn't want the life I saw around me: predictable, safe, and small. I tried to understand why I was here, who I was meant to be, and how to turn pain into something that mattered. That desire became both my compass and my undoing, leading me down a long, winding path toward becoming myself.

From the outside, my childhood looked perfect. Family portraits in our Sunday best hanging on my grandparents' living room wall, all smiles—a mother, a father, a son, and a daughter. My father was a nuclear reactor operator: intelligent, skilled, and highly paid. My mother stayed home, not by her own choice, devoted to her children and determined to help us live up to our full potential, a task that wasn't easy, since both my brother and I were classified as "gifted" in our formative years. She was busy because we got bored easily and were voracious for knowledge, experiences, and information about the world around us.

When I was eight, my parents built their dream house on an 11.5-acre lot in the middle of nowhere: two stories with a full basement, vaulted ceilings, floor-to-ceiling windows, exposed wood beams, and views from the ridge that could make a nature lover out of anyone. But pictures of the perfect family in the ideal house with breathtaking ridgetop views only tell the story people want to believe, the parts we let them know.

Inside that beautiful house, a very different story unfolded. It was a place of torment, heartbreak, and unspeakable chaos that left us living in fear for years, until my father's death in 2024 finally closed a chapter I'd been trying to rewrite my whole life.

Only a select few who knew us back then can truly understand what we endured—and what we escaped—thanks to my extraordinary mother. Fierce, determined, and fearless, she fought for our freedom with a courage that defied the odds. It wasn't a contest, but she won. She triumphed over torment, abuse, and fear. She saved the three of us.

And, in a way, she saved my father, too, though he never knew it. He never saw the hell he had escaped, never understood that if we had stayed, one of us might have been driven to take drastic action just for a chance to be free. He would have "won" by shaping us in his image, trapping us in his relentless mind games for eternity, but she stopped that. Because of her, we survived, and we became whole on our own, free from his clutches.

My mother is a hero, though she would never claim the title, so I am claiming it for her. People should know who she really is and the life she made possible for my brother and me. I will never forget it, and I will never stop being grateful for the freedom, the courage, and the future she fought to give us.

As an adult looking back, I don't remember it being terrifying all the time. I remember fishing and canoeing trips with my dad, squealing and shrieking loudly when the worm wrapped itself around my finger as I tried to put it on the hook, making my father laugh until he coughed so hard that he had to put down his cigarette. Making him laugh felt like victory. It made me glad to hear him laugh or see him smile, because it was pretty rare.

My dad always seemed sad, and I could never really figure out why, even after I grew up and tried to understand him as an adult many years later. All I ever hoped was that I could make it better, that he could love me like other little girls' fathers. That he would be proud of me and comfort me like those dads you see on television, beaming with pride for their daughters as they graduate, get married, come home from college, or celebrate a fantastic milestone.

But not my dad. His straight-A, honor-roll-student daughter was never good enough. I could read at three, write my name in cursive before kindergarten, play sports with the boys because there were no girls' leagues in our small town, and shoot a Winchester rifle with outstanding accuracy for a young southern girl (I even won a county turkey shoot one year at Thanksgiving). I was runner-up in a county-wide basketball foul-shot competition against high schoolers at the age of nine.

I immersed myself in all of these non-gender-normative activities—not for myself, but to shift the focus away from my first best friend, my dearest brother. It was my way of shielding him, of giving him space to be himself, while I explored the edges and gently tested the waters of who I was allowed to be. He is five years and two days older than me, so he was always looking out for me, and this was my only way, being the youngest, to return the favor. My brother came home from school every day and taught me what he learned because I wanted to know everything he did, and he wanted me to as well. Our own language and shorthand grew from necessity, a private thread of connection that endured through the years—impossible for anyone else to understand, impossible for us to fully explain. My brother has always been a cerebral, thoughtful, and beautiful soul, full of intelligence, insight, and an overwhelming depth of knowledge. Back then, people in our small town just called him weird. He struggled both at home and at school, and he was never what my father considered a "typical" boy. He was smart, intellectual, not sporty, and never really fit in anywhere, except with me.

To keep my brother safe, I stepped into the roles my father expected, filling every perceived gender gap. I played sports, went on fishing and canoeing trips, and tried to meet his idea of a "typical" child—all while shielding my brother from what I knew could harm him. Unfortunately, this also meant my father favored me.

My father never physically hit me, but he did psychologically torture me, constantly manipulating my undying love for my mother and brother to get what he wanted. Sometimes, he forced me to trade my loyalty, to take his side when all I wanted was to stand up to him. As a young child, I made these exchanges—sometimes to keep him temporarily calm, to prevent him from drinking or acting out, to delay the violence just long enough to survive the night. In those small, tense victories, I quietly shared the spoils of psychological warfare—gifts he paraded as mine alone—with my mother and brother, a fragile reminder that we were still connected and protected in the midst of his cruelty.

I remember the first time I wished for a different life than the one I had. The first moment I truly realized there had to be more out there for me. I was about eight years old. I had just played in an elementary-school basketball game, scored several baskets, and helped my team win. But that wasn't good enough for my father. He yelled at me in the car the whole way home for not playing enough defensive offense, for not "getting in there with elbows" when I had the ball. I was the highest-scoring player on my team, and still, it wasn't enough. It was never enough.

While my mother and brother argued with him to keep attention off me—a move we choreographed over the years to precision perfection—I tuned out the noise in the car. Tears streamed down my face as I tried to catch my breath, as I had done so many times before. But this time was different. I knew this was not the life I wanted for myself as I got older.

The moon was exceptionally bright and beautiful that night. I saw one star, the first I saw that evening, shining particularly bright, and I remembered and mouthed words to myself:

Starlight, star bright, first star I see tonight.

I wish I may, I wish I might, have this wish I wish tonight.

My wish was simple. I had to grow up and get away from this: the fighting, the yelling, the crying, the chaos. The drunken or drug-induced rants, the fists, slamming my mother into door frames, throwing her down stairs, my father locking my brother in the bathroom and then beating him in the bathtub while my mom and I tried to break the door down, my father drunkenly shooting shotguns off the back deck outside my bedroom window at 2:00 a.m., blasting music at all hours because he was high and wanted to "have some fun." No child should ever have to live like this. I became a master at becoming invisible, hiding in closets and under tables to stay away from his rages.

So I made my wish. I wished on that star that I would grow up and move away from my hometown, go to college even if I had to take out loans, begin a career, be successful, and never take anything from my father, marry a man who would adore me—not just love me but *adore* me—and never treat my mom and brother this way. I wished to build a house of my own and fill it with animals, people I love, and peace.

Spoiler: It all came true.

My starry-night wish stayed with me, tucked in my chest like a secret talisman. Every day after that, I carried it quietly, a small flame in the middle of chaos. It wasn't just a wish; it was a contract with myself. I would survive. I would leave. And I would build a life that honored the people I loved and protected, especially my mother and brother.

It was the first step on a long road—not measured in miles, but in moments of awakening, in choices that would define who I would become. In that moment, I realized something powerful: Hope begins the moment we decide our story isn't over.

School became more than a place to learn; it became a lifeline. Every assignment, every grade, every teacher's encouragement, and every small achievement were reminders that I could exist beyond the walls of that house. I threw myself into academics, cheerleading, singing, and anything that allowed me to prove, at least to myself, that I was capable of more.

By the time I was thirteen, the escape my mother and I had discussed for years finally began. Quietly and courageously, my mother had saved enough money to make it possible. We got out the checkbook for the secret account and looked at our balance. We had enough money to get away. It was finally time. The timing of our escape could not have been more precarious: My maternal grandmother was dying of colon cancer, and the window to make a move was short. My mother, brother, and I moved in with her so my mother could care for her during her final months. It was the perfect opportunity, a bittersweet opening, to leave the life that had tried to define us and step into the unknown. I hope she knew how much her end was also our beginning, a new life and hope that emerged from the ache of losing her, our biggest fan and cheerleader. She would be so proud of my mother and of who my brother and I have become.

Even then, leaving wasn't easy. My father had kept my mother from working when they were together, controlling her every move, so she had to find work for the first time in years. The money she had saved wasn't nearly enough to sustain us: "Budget-conscious" doesn't even begin to describe our situation.

My father had us followed all over our small town by his friends, private investigators, and even random acquaintances he met at bars. They would park down the street for hours, watching our house. He would frequently show up at my grandmother's home in the middle of the night, pounding on doors, yelling like a madman, his loud, drunken voice echoing across the neighborhood.

He still tormented us, but this time, it was different. There was an odd sense of peace in knowing he was outside the house we now lived in, unable to reach us. I knew he would eventually tire himself out, like a toddler having a tantrum, and leave.

Fear still followed us like a shadow, but so did hope. The air inside and outside the house, the freedom of sitting on the porch swing at my grandmother's, listening to my Walkman in peace when our followers weren't around, and the dawning realization that the world extended beyond our small town were intoxicating and terrifying all at once. In that strange mix of grief, escape, and relief, I began to feel something I had never allowed myself to feel before: possibility.

Though the road ahead was uncertain, one thing was clear: Our story wasn't over. That secret wish I had made under the bright night sky was still alive, guiding me toward the life I would choose. Every step, every choice, every quiet triumph along the way was proof that hope could survive even the darkest beginnings.

That starlight wish became a promise to myself.

2

The Spark and the Shadows

Pain doesn't always transform us through enlightenment. Sometimes it fuels us—quietly, fiercely—until we've built something strong enough to stand on.

My early twenties were a storm. In 2001, I moved to Knoxville with a friend from my two-year private college, thrilled to finally step into adulthood. I had a place of my own, even if it was shared, and a new chapter waiting to be written. I loved the pulse of the city, the hum of possibility in every streetlight and lecture hall. There was freedom in the anonymity, in going to class, blending into crowds, and realizing that no one around me knew who I was or where I came from. No one cared. After years of being watched, followed, and controlled by my father, that simple indifference felt like a revelation.

In 2002, I had been seeing someone for over a year, and on the surface, everything seemed good. We laughed easily, shared late-night drives and plans for the future—the kind of comfort I thought meant love. When his grandparents invited me to join them on a trip to Aruba, I was thrilled. They offered to cover everything if I could only pay for my plane ticket—fair trade, I thought, a chance to see turquoise water, to finally exhale.

But paradise has a way of exposing what's already cracking beneath the surface. What should have been a dream vacation turned into a blur of arguments and uneasy silences. There was yelling, then lots of drinking— mine, mostly—to numb the noise and pretend we were okay.

When I returned from the trip, I was exhausted and ready to slip back into the rhythm of daily life: classes, work, homework squeezed into every spare moment. But when I unlocked the door to my apartment, I froze. The living room was empty. Every piece of my roommate's furniture was gone. No warning, no note, no conversation—just absence. She had moved out while I was out of the country, leaving me to walk into the hollow quiet of an apartment that no longer felt like home. When I called her, she barely said a word, just mentioned that she'd moved in with her new boyfriend across the hallway. I never spoke to her again.

I couldn't afford to live alone—not even in the cheapest apartment my roommate and I had rented. Luckily, I'd always been a saver. I had just enough to cover the next month's rent, but after that, I had no idea what I would do. So I called my boyfriend, who had mentioned wanting to move out of his grandparents' house anyway, and asked if he'd consider moving in with me— at least temporarily, until I could get back on my feet. He agreed. What started as a short-term solution turned into nearly two years of living together.

It all worked—until a late-night conversation in 2004 left me hollow and unsure of who I was without the version of myself I had built around someone I thought was *the one*—the one I would marry, the one I had wished for all those years ago. But he was neither of those things.

One night, after working a double shift at a residential psychiatric facility for children, I came home exhausted. We were short-staffed, and the work was both grueling and rewarding. A double shift could drain the life out of anyone, especially after an hour-long drive. I finally stumbled in around 2:00 a.m. and slipped into bed beside him, thinking he was asleep.

Then, out of the dark, came his voice:

"I'm moving out tomorrow."

After more than two years together, after conversations about weddings and shared futures, he broke up with me in the dark, in the middle of the night. *Seriously?*

I sat up, turned on the lamp, and said, "I hope you don't think I am going to let you sleep now. Why wait until tomorrow? You can pack and leave right now. Oh, and I'm keeping the cat."

I was furious. Most of what was in the apartment was mine anyway, so there wasn't much to lose, but the betrayal stung. I watched him pack, tears burning my eyes, my body trembling from shock. Yet, even in that moment, part of me began to shift. Here was another example of someone who couldn't give me what I wanted—or what I deserved. And somehow, that realization was its own kind of clarity.

It was just me now—and my sweet boy, Kitty, the tiny barn-born kitten who had no idea how much I needed him. Cats had always been my constant, and I refused to let him take that from me, too.

For months after the breakup, I threw myself into partying with friends, trying to drown the silence with laughter, the pain with alcohol, and the loneliness with noise. But by the following year, after months of outrunning myself, I finally found a moment of truth.

It was a Saturday evening, and I was sitting on the porch of my Knoxville apartment, drinking wine with a friend after another night of reckless partying. I remember turning to her, my voice slurred and heavy with honesty, and saying, "I don't know what I'm doing anymore. This isn't me. I can't end up like my father. I don't want to be this person. I'm done."

Shortly after that night, I left my master's program to become a therapist, a dream that suddenly felt too heavy to chase. Not long after, my paternal grandfather died unexpectedly in 2005, shaking the ground beneath me once again. He was the Pappaw to my Feeterpee, my steady anchor through the storms of childhood, and his loss left my paternal grandmother adrift, recovering from a heart attack soon after his passing. I stepped in to care for her, though my father, living just minutes away, did nothing.

The last time I spoke to my father was in 2009, just before I married Michael. It was a futile attempt to see if he could be supportive, caring, or kind. By then, I had spent four years caring for his mother after my grandfather passed. Every Saturday, I got up early, no matter how late I'd gotten home the night before. I stopped at Bojangles for biscuits and drove an hour to her house. I spent the day cleaning and helping her take a bubble bath—her simplest joy. I took her grocery shopping and to the local beauty school, making sure her hair was exactly how she liked it. I stocked her fridge with strawberries she couldn't afford, organized her kitchen as her senses faded in her nineties. Those Saturdays were a labor of love and a gift I will never regret.

As my wedding neared, my father reached out, ostensibly to contact my mother about a portion of their divorce settlement. I saw it as an opportunity to attempt a relationship with him before my wedding, fueled by a mix of hope and naive idealism. The hope that someone might magically get their act together long enough to show up.

We met a few times. Some encounters were relatively peaceful. He even took my fiancé and me out for dinner once. For a brief moment, I allowed myself to think he might have a place in my life. But I remained cautious. I had tried this, in some form or another, for the fifteen years since my parents' divorce, and it had never ended well. I knew better than to let my guard down completely.

Then, as always, it ended.

I was driving home from work one afternoon when I got a call from him. We talked about small things—our days, his recent email to my mother about the settlement, a couple of errands I was running for the wedding—life things. I mentioned that Michael and I were planning to move to Florida after we got married, and that he needed a plan to care for his mother. And then, suddenly, he cut me off completely—the abrupt, familiar telltale sign of the end.

But it wasn't just abrupt. It was cruel. He told me my grandfather, the man who had called me Feeterpee and constantly beamed with pride at me, his only granddaughter, would be ashamed of me for "abandoning" my grandmother.

Then, with finality that left no room for argument, he said, "Why don't you just move to Florida and have a nice fucking life?"

The last words I ever said to my father were simple. Calm. Certain.

"Don't you worry. I plan on it."

And I did. I never looked back. And I never spoke to my father again.

In that instant, the weight of his control lifted. Relief flooded me. Resolve steadied me. Clarity sharpened my vision. The world he had tried to trap me in no longer had any hold.

It was my turning point, though I didn't recognize it at the time. I was reclaiming my power. It was the moment I realized I didn't owe him my pain, my guilt, or my silence.

Each loss, each disappointment from those years, added fuel to a quiet fire I didn't yet fully understand. I wasn't thinking about healing or purpose; I was thinking only about survival. I wanted to prove that I could rise, that I could thrive, and that I could build a life that was mine, untouched by anyone else's limitations or expectations. Deep down, I wanted to prove to my father, the man who fractured so much of my early world, that I could do everything without him. Better than him. And I did.

When I thought of success, I thought of it as armor. Degrees, promotions, independence—they weren't just achievements; they were declarations. *You don't get to define me anymore.* Every late night of studying, every risk I took, every time I pushed through exhaustion, it was powered by something primal. Not peace. Not healing. Just the relentless desire to overcome.

In the years that followed, that quiet fire never went out. It became my drive, my ambition, my edge. I built my life brick by brick, fueled by purpose, by the quiet discovery of my own peace. And somewhere along the way, the need to prove something transformed into something gentler: the desire to become someone I respected, and to build something I was proud of.

Because maybe that's what overcoming really is: not forgetting where you came from, but choosing, over and over, to build something beautiful on the ashes, rising in grace and authenticity, like a phoenix.

Even then, though I hadn't yet learned the art of reframing pain, a seed had been planted: Maybe nothing is wasted—not hurt, not loss, not disappointment.

3

The Reframe

Even before I could name it, I had always been a radical optimist at my core. Not the kind of optimism that ignores reality or pretends pain doesn't exist, but the type that chooses to see possibility, even when the world around me seemed determined to close every door. It was a stubborn, quiet spark, one that carried me through heartbreak, loss, and countless challenges long before I could consciously call it reframing.

I learned to see possibilities early, finding small ways to shift perspective while comforting my brother after one of my father's explosions of rage, once again placing my hand on his chest to calm him while he sobbed. Those terrifying moments shattered any illusion of peace in our childhood, leaving us clinging to each other for solace.

Yet, in the wreckage of fear and chaos, we discovered something extraordinary: a bond built through survival, and a fragile but unyielding belief that the world could be different, that we would survive it, and somehow, maybe even find beauty within it.

That spark became my compass. It guided me through the uncertainty of adolescence, the loneliness of leaving home, and the tempest of young adulthood. Even when I felt crushed by disappointment or betrayed by someone I trusted, there was a quiet voice within me whispering, *There is another way to see this, another choice to make.* It wasn't always easy to follow, and it wasn't always obvious, but that little spark—that stubborn insistence on possibility—never went out. I was experiencing radical optimism.

Radical optimism, I would come to realize, isn't about denying pain or pretending life is fair. It's about seeing what *is,* acknowledging the worst, and still choosing to believe in what *could be.* It's about taking the ashes of what has been and daring to build something better. And in my life, that choice has been both my grounding and my wings.

My thirties and early forties didn't bring any sudden, mystical awakening. They brought *life:* responsibility, disappointment, and the messy, beautiful work of figuring out how to live authentically while holding on to the optimism that had always lived inside me.

Life was in full force: the work of standing tall in my own strength, fully inhabiting the world I had built with Michael, my fiercely supportive husband, who always believes in me and my wildest dreams. We didn't have children through no fault of our own, but family was ever-present. After my mother's stroke, she moved in with us in Florida. Though the circumstances were challenging, my optimism whispered possibilities: *I can make her feel safe, comfortable, and loved in a way she hasn't experienced in years. I can create moments of joy despite the limitations of her recovery.*

She was fortunate: Only a rare, gentle slip of words remained as a reminder of what she'd endured. No physical limitations, no loss of spirit. Just resilience. We were grateful for her recovery, for our time together, and for the quiet reminder that hope can rebuild what fear once tried to destroy.

Most of Michael's family was nearby, and we cared for his grandparents several days a week until they passed. Some days were exhausting. Some were heartbreaking. But even then, my optimism quietly surfaced: These hours of care, small and sometimes tedious, were *meaningful.* They built connection, trust, and memory. They taught patience, humility, and gratitude. Even in loss, I noticed opportunity—to love deeply, to grow, and to be present when it mattered most.

I'll never forget playing games with his grandparents, being surprised by their sharp wit and endless knowledge, and remembering from my own grandparents just how fleeting time with loved ones can be. Each shared meal, each wheelchair ride to lunch, each visit to the rehab facility after Poolie's leg amputation—these were *priceless moments*. They welcomed me, loved me as their own, and even called me their granddaughter when speaking with friends and caretakers. It meant the world to me to have grandparents again.

After Michael's grandparents both passed, we moved to Colorado to start a new chapter, building a home, a life, and a space where our chosen family could thrive. A few years later, a health scare brought my brother to live with us, adding another layer of connection, care, and shared life under one roof. Each adjustment required energy, flexibility, and sacrifice, but my optimism always whispered: *We can figure this out. We can make it work. We can build a home that is loving, peaceful, and purposeful.*

And somewhere in the middle of all that change, I realized something unexpected: I could actually *enjoy* the process.

Professionally, these decades were marked by relentless growth. I excelled in city, county, and state government public assistance, establishing myself as a leader in state policy. But eventually, as it always has throughout my career, a period of stagnation set in. I applied for higher-level roles repeatedly, only to be passed over as the *second choice* every time. For someone who had always achieved what she set her mind to, it was exasperating. I felt stuck. Something had to change, and this time I realized it had to be *me*.

I had long been haunted by not finishing my master's degree—I withdrew with only two semesters left because the path hadn't felt right. But in that moment of reflection, I thought, *Why the hell not go ahead and get a master's degree? It's always bothered me. I'm going to go for it. It could be really fun.*

In 2022, I enrolled in an MBA program at Western Governors University and graduated in 2023. I completed a two-year program in one year while working full-time, earning awards for my performance. I "mastered" it—yes, a terrible pun, but it makes me smile as I write this. It validated the knowledge I'd spent years building and reminded me that nothing is in my way now. I am no longer holding myself back.

From there, I transitioned into public assistance, technology, and eventually contracted with a Fortune Top Five company in employee experience. Each role demanded focus, strategy, and the ability to guide others with vision and purpose. And through every transition, my optimism didn't fade; in fact, it *fueled* me. It helped me see opportunity where others saw only obstacles. When colleagues doubted the path forward, I saw nothing but potential. When systems felt broken, I saw possibility. I led with a steady confidence that solutions could be found, that progress could happen, and that our efforts mattered.

Long before I could name the practice, I was already reframing—choosing my response over the circumstance, holding space for what was difficult without letting it define me, and quietly turning challenge into possibility. Caregiving, career pivots, relocations, and integrating family into our home all became exercises in seeing differently. Each moment, each hardship, was an invitation to notice what could be salvaged, to turn difficulty into growth.

Each small act of optimism—taking my mother to a doctor's appointment expecting great results, finding an innovative solution to a problem at work, building new routines for our home—became a quiet assertion: *We can thrive, even here, even now.*

By the end of this period, I understood one truth: Radical optimism isn't naive thinking. It's survival. It's leadership.

It's the ability to guide myself and others through uncertainty and loss, to transform obstacles into pathways, and to quietly reclaim agency in a world that often feels chaotic.

Reframe Practice: Radical Optimism
Think back to a moment in your life that once felt impossible, painful, or limiting.

Now, look at it through a new lens and write down your reflections:
What hidden opportunities did it carry?
What strength did it awaken in you?
How did it quietly prepare you for something better?

Let yourself feel the spark of possibility—that quiet, radical optimism that's always lived inside you—while you write.

18

II

Part Two

*As I grew older, the lessons of those early years followed me
forward.*
*This was the stretch where effort became armor—where
achievement, adaptability, and resilience stood in for belonging. I
learned how to perform competence, how to keep going, how to
survive by becoming useful. This part traces the years of striving,
when forward motion mattered more than reflection, and
becoming someone often meant moving away from myself.*

4

Performing

There are moments in childhood that never entirely leave the body. You grow up, build a life, build strength, and build a name—but something small from long ago still hums beneath the surface, shaping the way you breathe, the way you enter a room, the way you rise.

Before I ever stepped onto a school stage, there were Sundays in my grandfather's living room in 1983—Sundays steeped in strong coffee, cigarette smoke, and the low thrum of NASCAR or rodeo championships humming from the television. I was three years old, sitting cross-legged on the worn carpet or perched on my grandfather's lap, a newspaper spread open across my tiny hands. I could already read complete sentences by then. My brother had taught me everything he learned at school each afternoon, cheering me on with the kind of gentle patience kids rarely get from adults.

To many grown-ups, my reading was a novelty. During southern "visiting" hours—friends and neighbors drifting in after church—someone would inevitably say, "Read something for them." I'd lift the paper and read whatever they pointed to, their faces softening with surprise. They saw brilliance. I felt expectation. Even then, at only three, I scanned faces for safety: Are they smiling? Did I do it right? Am I enough? "Exceptional" became the mask I learned to wear long before I understood its weight.

Two years later, in kindergarten, that mask followed me under lights that felt too bright for such a small stage and a paper crown that sat crooked on my head. I had practiced my lines for days with the earnest determination of a five-year-old. When my mother knelt beside me in the parking lot, tucking a loose strand of hair behind my ear and telling me I was ready, I believed her. But when I stepped up to the podium, I could barely see over and scanned the crowd. My eyes went straight to my family.

My mother smiled. My brother leaned forward, proud. And then there was my father—arms folded, jaw tight, a familiar storm behind his expression. The words vanished from the page before I could speak them. Heat gathered in my face. Panic surged. And the tears came fast, sending me running backstage before I even understood I was moving.

I didn't understand it then, but I do now. That moment was less about the lines I forgot and more about the danger I felt in being visible. In our home, attention could shift the air. Mistakes had weight. Backstage, I sobbed as though I had broken something sacred. My mother gathered me into her arms, smoothing my hair, steadying my breath. She walked me back into the auditorium—not to perform, but to sit with her, to be held, to settle. I learned something wordless that day: Safety often lived outside the spotlight.

Years stretched forward from that moment, carrying me far from Tennessee to the edges of Florida's gulf. By 2010, I found myself stepping onto another stage—this time by choice, in a small community theater where the air smelled of sawdust and old velvet curtains. I had been cast as Sister James in *Doubt*, a role with no musical numbers to fold into, no chorus to blend with: just four actors, the sharp truth of the script, and the sound of my own breath.

One night, mid-scene, my mind went completely blank. The line evaporated. The lights sharpened around me. I felt the same tremor that once sent a five-year-old running, but something in me stayed rooted. The tremor rose, the echo of a child who once ran without thinking. But the woman I had become stayed in her body, remained in the scene, and stayed in the spotlight.

My acting partner caught the panic in my eyes and shifted his following line by a breath—so small the audience never noticed—offering me a lifeline disguised as improvisation. I inhaled. The words returned. The moment thinned like a storm drifting past. After the show, when friends told me they assumed the pause was intentional, I realized something I had never known:

Rising often begins because someone else holds the moment steady long enough for you to breathe again.

His support stayed with me long after the performance ended. It showed me how fear can evolve into strength when someone stands beside you, how vulnerability can become grounding, and how partnership can create a steadiness no amount of performance alone ever could.

Rising began to take on a different shape in my life after that. It showed up as the confidence to stand still when all I wanted to do was disappear. It showed up as pausing long enough to remain present, rather than falling into old patterns. It showed up as speaking to myself with the same gentleness I once saved only for others. It showed up as trusting that each step forward could be rooted in presence, not perfection. It showed up as learning to guide myself long before I ever tried to guide anyone else.

Rising is quiet. Subtle. A slow turning toward truth. It is opening your eyes to the moment you're in and listening for what it's teaching you. It is leaning a breath closer toward hope. It is standing with yourself instead of stepping away.

Rising begins within. And for me, it started in the very places where I first learned to shrink.

Reframe Practice—Staying With Yourself

Think of one moment when you felt small. Not to reopen it, but to meet it with who you are now.

Place your hand on your heart and ask yourself, *Where can I stay present in a place I once wanted to run from?*

You don't need a perfect answer. Just a breath. A moment of honesty.

Notice what the steadiness feels like now.

Notice the softness you can offer yourself.

Notice the quiet strength that wasn't there before.

Then give yourself a simple, straightforward promise: *I can rise here.*

Because rising began the first time you stayed with yourself.

5

Beyond the Mask

For as long as I can remember, I have nervously scanned faces and held my breath until I see signs of approval, or at least no signs of danger. It's a survival instinct that began long before I had words for it. It kept me safe when my father went quiet after someone said something he didn't like, or when our family was forced to choose between him and the drinking and drugs. The day we told him we were leaving to move in with my grandmother if he couldn't change, he made his choice. We packed our things and left the home that would eventually burn to the ground—thirty years later, literally. I learned to read the room before entering it—tiptoeing past my father when he was drunk and passed out on the couch—so I wouldn't wake him and face his wrath. Over time, that instinct became a skill, and that skill became a mask.

The mask looked like confidence, competence, charm, and grace under pressure, but it felt like panic on the inside. It allowed me to speak at conferences, present at meetings, and perform in community theater, even though I was holding my breath until it was over. It got me promoted, praised, and trusted. But beneath it, I was constantly negotiating my worth. Every decision, accomplishment, and silence carried the unspoken question: *Was that enough?*

Then came a moment that told me I was enough, though it took me a second to let that truth in. I have had the privilege of working for someone who values authenticity immensely. One of the first times I realized the mask could fall and it would be okay was in a 1:1 with my boss. I made a quirky joke to lighten their tough week, softening it with, "Thanks for always letting me be my crazy, weirdo self." Their reply stunned me: "I don't actually find you weird or quirky. You are just right."

It just so happened that I wore one of my favorite sweatshirts to our next virtual meeting. It was purple—my favorite color—with the words "You are enough" on it. I often wear this sweatshirt when I am out in public to remind other people that they are enough, because I know what it feels like to need that reminder. When my boss saw it, they said, "Andrea, I love the shirt you are wearing. I hope you know you are not just enough. You are more than enough." I was stunned for a second, then laughed and joked, "Wait, is that a good thing?" Their reply shocked me, catching my breath with its weight: "It's a great thing. Against any weight or measure, you would never be found wanting."

After the call, I took off my headset, pushed back from my desk in my home office, put my face in my hands, and just cried. The pure acceptance was something I had never received from someone outside of my husband, mother, and brother—and if I had, no one had ever said it like that before. It healed a part of me, and I will never forget it.

That story became my mirror, the moment I finally saw who I had been hiding behind my mask all along. The reflection was far from perfect, but it was tender, vulnerable, and honest. Letting the mask slip had always felt unsafe to me, like walking into battle without armor. But when I showed up as my true self, I found connection in places I had once felt alone, even at work. The people who mattered most to me didn't need my performance—they wanted my presence. They wanted the real me, and now, I finally felt safe bringing her to work.

The mask I was wearing didn't make me strong; it made me a distilled version of myself, filtered by the audience around me. The more I face the reflection of who I really am and let the mask fall, the more I remember who I am—beyond approval, performance, hustle, and fear.

It takes practice to come out from behind the mask, especially when it's been up for a long time. Stepping into authenticity is something we learn gently, over time. Every moment I choose authenticity, I reclaim a piece of myself that was once hidden, silenced, or doubted.

Growth doesn't come from perfection; it comes from presence, courage, and the willingness to be fully seen.

Reframe Practice: Notice Where Your Mask Is Still Protecting Your Wound

You might think of a recent interaction where you felt tense, overprepared, or slightly "on." A moment when something in you felt guarded rather than at ease.

As you recall it, notice what mask you were wearing.
Was it confidence? Humor? Agreeableness? Competence?

Without judgment, you can gently ask yourself what that mask was protecting.
What fear or old habit might have been underneath?
Fear of judgment, rejection, or getting it wrong?

You may notice a quiet shift if you let the question change.

Instead of *How can I look perfect here?*
You might ask, *Who do I want to be in this moment?*

If it feels safe, you can experiment with one small opening next time.
Let one tiny edge of the mask loosen.
Share a thought, a quirk, or a feeling that feels real—even if it feels a little risky.

Afterward, take a moment to notice what changed.
What felt easier, lighter, or steadier?
Did the connection deepen?
Did you feel more seen—by someone else, or by yourself?

You can write down one small insight about what showing up more authentically offered you.

Daily Authenticity Prompt: Showing Your True Self

You might notice a moment today when you feel yourself putting on a mask.
Perhaps it shows up as confidence, humor, agreeableness, or the urge to be perfect.

When you catch it, you can pause and gently ask yourself, *Who do I want to be in this moment?*

From there, you might choose one small way to let a piece of your authentic self show.
It could be sharing a genuine thought or feeling.
It might be speaking your honest opinion.
Or allowing a quirk, a laugh, or a moment of vulnerability to appear.

Afterward, take a moment to notice how it felt.
Did you feel more present—more at ease?
More connected—to yourself or to someone else?

You can return to this prompt as often as it feels supportive, and notice how these small moments of honesty quietly build courage, presence, and trust.

6

Hollow Success

For years, I measured myself by results, accolades, successful performance, and external validation. I thought that to be accepted, successful, or valued, I had to achieve the highest title in an organization, the best grade as a student, and be the envy of everyone around me. Seeking this for so many years led to tight shoulders, shallow breathing, and a constant look over my shoulder for someone judging me, when I was actually judging myself.

Sitting on the porch swing at my grandmother's house, feeling the freedom of just being, I glimpsed who I could be when no one else's expectations controlled me. That spark—hope, tenacity, quiet rebellion—was always there, waiting for the right moment to guide me toward authenticity. I just hadn't yet learned that true fulfillment required showing up as myself, not hiding.

Ambition was my compass, and success was the map I followed during the earliest parts of my career, even when the journey didn't feel like mine. I thought proving myself would fill the emptiness left by childhood wounds, heartbreak, and parental absence. I was determined to succeed, to rise above, to be seen as capable, unstoppable, and undeniable.

I excelled in every role I took on and felt like the leader I knew I was in every industry I explored—nonprofit social services, behavioral health, hospitals, city, county, and state government public assistance—eventually leading in state policy and later moving into technology and corporate contracting, which was exhilarating. I could navigate complex systems, lead diverse teams, and solve problems others avoided, and it was thrilling to know I could get things done where others could not, but it still didn't feel like enough. On paper, I was a star. But inside, something was missing. I still felt stuck, thoroughly and completely exhausted. I began to get migraines frequently and carried knots in my shoulders that massage therapists couldn't work out.

Even as I climbed the professional ladder, echoes from my childhood stayed with me. I remembered hiding during my father's rages, quietly trying to make him laugh on fishing trips, protecting my brother whenever I could. Those early lessons in masking, vigilance, and surviving chaos became strategies I carried into adulthood. In every room—even in boardrooms and leadership meetings—I scanned for danger the same way I once did at home. I didn't yet realize how much of my professional presence was performance. When I presented to the human services board, I found they enjoyed my presentations most when I was the real me—not performing—just me cracking a joke and making them smile, even though I was presenting a regulation change to public policy, a seemingly boring topic. Moments like those gave me a glimpse of who I could be, but I didn't yet grasp how deeply I was performing as a professional.

I remember one leadership coaching session in particular. We were asked to take a short personality quiz. Having nearly completed a master's in psychology, I had taken Myers-Briggs, DiSC, and countless others. Hell, I had designed tests as part of my education. I thought I knew it all. So when I saw it was only twenty questions, I scoffed and thought: *Okay, sure. This will be fantastic. How can twenty questions possibly capture me in a statistically relevant way?*

A few weeks later, we reviewed our results individually. My coach greeted me with a smile and said he was shocked by my results. Shocked? By me? I assumed it was because I was remarkable—just as every result in my life had always indicated. And I was, just not in the way I had anticipated.

Then he showed me the two data columns from the assessment results: one for who I was at work and one for the real me. Seeing those numbers on the opposite ends of the scales from each other hit like a punch to the chest, and I immediately felt the tears rising in my eyes because I knew this was true. Once again, I was that kid in a house of chaos, shrinking to fit the room. I had been masking for so long, trying to fit a mold, that I forgot who I was underneath.

I sat there stunned, staring at the immense gap, and my stomach sank. I was slipping back into familiar patterns—masking, contorting myself to fit the room, trying to earn safety rather than inhabit it. These patterns were older than any role I had ever held. How could I have come so far to still be in the same place?

Behind my drive to succeed and my eagerness to please, I had been taught by both family and the workplace that showing my authentic self wasn't safe because I could see the faces in the room were displeased. Fun at work? A liability. Humor? Unprofessional. Quirkiness? Dangerous. I consider myself a high-functioning, masking neurodivergent individual, and as I had done around my father to stay safe, I had become excellent at hiding myself. I had learned to adjust quickly as a means of survival. But now, it was undeniable: Ambition without authenticity feels hollow.

On paper, I achieved. I got promotions, recognition, and accolades. But inside, I felt invisible. I was constantly performing—anticipating expectations, smoothing edges, and presenting the "right" version of myself—while my true self sat quietly in the corner, waiting to be seen.

I began noticing the difference between *performing* and *belonging.* I could shine, but I was holding my breath and didn't always feel seen. My work ethic, perseverance, and capability were admired, but my ideas, humor, and values often went unnoticed. I remember an executive leader complimenting a project I had managed successfully. As thrilled as I was to be recognized, it felt so hollow because that person also responded with annoyance when I had a moment of authenticity in front of them. I had built a life that looked like success but felt borrowed, shaped by everyone else's expectations.

It wasn't until the quiet moments—sitting on the back porch of our Colorado home, watching another colorful sunset behind the hills, or watching my mother rebuild her life with quiet grace while I beamed with pride at how far she had come—that I chose to push forward. This was not to impress anyone, but to honor my own path. My worth wasn't in the degree, the promotion, the compliment, or the award. My worth was in showing up authentically, in letting others see the real me, edges and all.

When I began weaving my voice, ideas, and principles into my work, leadership became effortless. Influence felt natural. Fulfillment arrived quietly, almost imperceptibly, but unmistakably. My ambition didn't disappear; it evolved. It became intentional, aligned, and fueled by purpose rather than validation, and finding fulfillment with purpose made the journey that much more rewarding.

Looking back, the hollow achievements were never the problem; they were the lesson. They taught me what it feels like to chase success without soul, to prove worth without connection, and to excel without alignment. And in learning that lesson, I found the path forward: one where proving myself wasn't about showing the world what I could do but showing *myself* who I could be when I stood firmly in my own truth.

Even small, everyday moments mattered: releasing stress through laughter with a colleague, the pride of recommending a new approach no one else dared, finding a way to bring humor to a tense situation, or simply allowing my quirky self to exist in the workplace. It felt radical in its simplicity. These small acts built the bridge between performing and belonging, between ambition and authenticity.

By showing up authentically, I realized that my quiet spark of optimism—knowing what I had survived and that if hope can last even after all of that—could guide me just as powerfully in the professional world as it had in my personal one. It was time to get to work on making it happen.

But as I grew older, I traded that quiet clarity for something louder—ambition. Ambition became my compass.

Reflection Exercise: Finding Your True Self

Think about a time when you chased success, recognition, or approval at the expense of your true self.

What did that experience teach you?

How might success feel and look if it were built on authenticity rather than performance?

What's one small step you could take today to let the real you be seen?

7

The Becoming

For most of my life, I chased perfection. Not because I loved the idea of being flawless, as tempting yet unattainable as that is, but because I was trained to believe that anything less than perfect was unacceptable and the only way to be lovable. Mistakes were dangerous, vulnerability was weakness, and asking for help was a sign of failure and disappointment. I performed, polished, and masked—not just for others, but for myself—creating an impossible illusion no one could ever reach. In my becoming, some moments shattered that illusion to bits.

When I was about nine years old, I proudly bounded home one day to announce another straight-A report card. My father took one look, peered over the top of the cardstock, and I immediately saw what was coming. He yelled for hours, even across the dinner table, over the one A- on the report card. It was absurd and extreme, and as an adult, I can see how ridiculous it was. It was still an A, but to him, an A- was shameful. His laser focus on the one tiny thing that was slightly imperfect on a card swimming with excellence made my heart sink and stomach drop. That moment, frozen in my memory, captured the beginning of a lifetime habit: striving for perfection in the hopes of earning approval that would never come.

Decades later, I carried that habit of approval-seeking into the workplace, smoothing edges and apologizing for things that were never mine to own. I led a large virtual meeting one day and apologized for someone else's absence, even calling myself the "humble replacement." After the call, a trusted friend and colleague pulled me aside and said words that hit me like a bolt of lightning, her stern tone taking my breath away:

"Stop apologizing. You have absolutely nothing to apologize for. You undermine yourself when you do that. STOP APOLOGIZING! You are awesome."

She helped me see that, for all those years, I had internalized a childhood pattern that no longer served me as an adult. I apologized to stay safe and make everyone happy, but as an adult, that made me feel less credible and confident. I began allowing myself to be human, to make mistakes, to speak my mind without preemptive apology, to stop undermining the value of what I had to say, and to embrace imperfection as part of growth.

I realized vulnerability was no longer a weakness—it was leadership. Being fully human allowed connection to take hold, built trust and rapport with my colleagues, and made me more effective. I practiced finding new ways to integrate authenticity into every interaction from that day forward.

If you feel the pull to perform flawlessly, pause, take a breath, and ask yourself: *Who do I want to be for them?* Not the polished version. Not the version that hides errors or fears. The human version: curious, courageous, and honest. What would that human version of you look like?

Reframe Practice: Being Human

You might notice how often the question *What will they think of me?* quietly takes the lead.

You can gently offer yourself a different question instead: *Who do I want to be for them?*

When you allow yourself to be fully human, something shifts.

Courage becomes less about performance and more about presence.

You begin choosing honesty over comfort, and showing up as you are—flaws included.

You might reflect on one recent moment when fear of judgment held you back.
What could have changed if you had shown up as your authentic self instead?
What is one small way you could practice leading from your humanity today?

Daily Courage Prompt

You might notice a moment today when fear, judgment, or perfectionism shows up.

If it feels right, you can choose one small action that reflects who you truly are.
It could be speaking up, sharing an idea, letting go of an unnecessary apology, or allowing a small mistake to stand.

At the end of the day, you can take a moment to notice how it felt.

III

Part Three

Eventually, the ways I had learned to survive began to ask for more than they could give.
This was not a sudden breaking, but a gradual reckoning—a series of moments when the old rules stopped working and the noise grew harder to ignore. Questions surfaced where certainty once lived. This section holds the unraveling, the pauses, and the first quiet realizations that something truer was waiting beneath the effort.

8

The Bridge Between Then and Now

Some bridges in life are so quiet you don't realize you've crossed them until you look back and see the distance between who you were and who you've become. They rarely arrive as dramatic turning points or milestones. They form one choice at a time, each event shaping you into the person who emerges on the other side.

One of those bridges began for me while I worked in a residential psychiatric facility for children near Knoxville, long before I understood I was healing myself while trying to help others.

The facility housed children who had already endured more heartbreak than most adults ever would. They had witnessed the worst kinds of parental neglect and violence, carrying burdens far too heavy for their ages. Sudden noises or raised voices made some of them flinch. Others protected themselves with silence, and some with fury. I called them "my kids"—not because they belonged to me, but because something in them felt familiar. Their fear. Their old souls shaped by too much life too soon. They hoped someone steady would stay—someone who felt like warmth after so much cold.

Morning shifts meant arriving before sunrise while the night staff waited in metal folding chairs lined along the hallway. The building carried a quiet that felt both sacred and heavy. Once the shift changed over, I sang—old jazz, showtunes, soft love songs—letting the notes drift through the corridor to let the children know it was time to start the day. It came from instinct instead

41

of a pressure to perform, a simple way of saying, "You're safe. I'm here. You matter."

My morning songs brought faint laughter or stirring sometimes, stillness at others. Yet the ritual held. When the kids stepped into the hallway with sleep still softening their faces, it felt like a small ceremony for a new day. Years later, I understood the fuller truth: The mornings I created for them were the mornings I still needed myself. While singing to them, I was also singing to the girl I had once been.

Healing often moves sideways like that—quiet, steady, and almost unnoticed. It grows in the moments when you offer someone else what you once longed for. At times, healing arrives in a single sharp moment that breaks something open. One afternoon, an eighteen-year-old who was days from aging out of the facility learned in a therapy session that her parents refused to take her back. No conversation or softness. A cold dismissal that split her world. Rage rose fast, hard, and desperate. She swung at the nearest person, which happened to be me. Her fist cracked against my cheek while staff rushed toward us to hold her against the wall and prevent another physical outburst. For me, something deeper revealed itself beneath her fury.

I stepped toward her with care and asked the only question that surfaced: "I know that wasn't about me. Who are you really mad at?" Her anger collapsed into grief. She sobbed into the summer air while her entire body trembled. When the surge passed, I guided her outside to walk across the property— past the trees, past the worn patches of earth where the kids played—and led her to a quiet spot where we all went to breathe on occasion. We talked about fear, adult choices, the life she deserved, and the life she could still build. Somewhere between her words and mine, something in me softened, and we met each other with the gentleness we both needed.

After the hardest days at the facility—when trauma moved through the halls, and a child's pain filled the air—I drove home with the radio turned up too loud, trying to quiet the echoes long enough to reach my apartment.

Kitty always found me wherever I landed in the apartment. He climbed into my lap or stretched out beside me the moment I stopped moving, pressing his soft body against mine and purring with a steady, familiar sound. He had been with me through heartbreak, long workdays, lonely seasons, and the slow rebuilding that came after each setback. Now he was grounding me in a way I needed more than I understood.

My childhood taught me how to read a room. Early adulthood taught me how to be steady for others when their emotions spilled over. This season taught me how to be constant for myself. Supporting those kids showed me my strength. Creating safety for them revealed what safety could feel like in my body. Sitting with their grief made room for me to acknowledge mine. I began to understand that the child I had been, and the woman I was becoming, were part of the same story.

Leadership revealed itself as something steady and human. It meant paying attention. It meant staying when someone needed support. It meant telling a child—or an adult—that they deserved gentleness, even in challenging moments. I saw it in morning songs and in late-night conversations that eased fear, and I gradually began treating myself with the same care I offered others. It showed up in friendships, in family, in marriage, and in the quiet places where people grow together.

When I look back now, the connection between then and now is clear. Every child I held space for held space for me in return. Every moment of softness reached something that needed softening in me. Every time I steadied someone else, my steadiness grew. That season taught me how to lead with compassion, how to move through the world without performing, and how to hold my own story with clarity and care.

Reframe Practice: The Quiet Bridge

You might think of a moment this week when you softened for someone else.
As you recall it, notice what that moment echoed inside you.

You may find steadiness in a small ritual that grounds you—a song,

a breath, a quiet pause.
Something simple you can return to, again and again, as a way of anchoring your day.

You might picture a younger version of yourself who needed gentleness.
If it feels right, you can offer them one sentence of reassurance.
You may also remember a recent moment when you stayed present for someone else.
Take a moment to acknowledge how that presence strengthened you, too.

Finally, you might name one quiet bridge you're crossing right now.
Even if the shift feels small.
Even if it's only beginning to take shape.

9

The Pressure That Changed Everything

Pressure has a way of revealing what you've carried for far too long. It gathers slowly, almost invisibly, until one day, your body tells the truth before your mind can catch up. That's what happened to me, and to so many others, when COVID hit in 2020, and the world shifted overnight, leaving every familiar routine behind.

My days blurred into emergency meetings, shifting federal guidance, and decisions that carried far more weight than my home office could hold. Each hour brought new updates. Leadership wanted answers, staff needed direction, and families depended on systems that were bending under pressure none of us expected. I woke with dread, felt a tightness behind my ribs most of the afternoon, and ended every day struggling to take a full breath.

On camera, I looked steady, composed, in control.

Off camera, my hands shook.

The panic attacks came without warning—the sudden rush of cold, the racing heart, the sense that the room was shrinking, and the desperate fight for breath that never seemed to let up. I had always been the grounded one, the person others leaned on. Now I sat between meetings with my camera off, trying to calm a body that refused to cooperate.

Eventually, I reached my limit. My doctor listened closely as I tried to describe the fogginess in my mind, the way my breath kept catching, and the constant hum of a nervous system that would not settle. I left with a diagnosis of generalized anxiety disorder and clinical depression. Medication became part of my routine. Getting help wasn't a weakness; it was a return to stability.

I wasn't doing any of this alone. My husband checked on me throughout the day, adding water to my desk when the glass sat empty or bringing me something small to eat when the hours slipped by. My mom lived with us then and could hear the strain in my voice as meetings stacked on top of one another. She stepped into my doorway sometimes to make sure I was steady. And although my brother was still in Tennessee, he sent texts that reminded me I was loved and that the weight of that year did not go unnoticed.

On nights when everything settled too heavily in my chest, Kitty curled against me the moment I sat down. His purr had a grounding rhythm I leaned into more than I realized. Their presence—each in their own way—gave me enough stability to face the next day.

Still, even with all that support, some evenings the pressure had nowhere to go. I closed my laptop and lay across the bed, overwhelmed by a nervous system that had carried more than it should. I placed my hands on my chest and tried to steady my breath, whispering to myself with a kindness I rarely directed inward. Michael would come in, find me lying there, and lie beside me. These moments were about genuine care: medication, support, rest, and the slow work of finding my way back to myself.

Over time, something shifted in small, steady movements. I slept a little deeper. My breath settled more quickly after an attack. I learned to pause rather than push through. I stopped performing steadiness and began building it. My family stayed close, loving me through the parts I was still learning to understand but could not always explain verbally.

By the time life began to settle again, I felt more grounded than I had in years. Then, in 2024, my father died.

The sadness that surfaced wasn't about losing a parent. It was for the possibility I had carried as a child—the imagined version of him who might have aged into a safer presence, a softer heart, and the capacity to be a dad instead of a father. I remembered the moment he said he wished I had never been born and how sharply that sentence lodged inside me. I remembered him telling me I couldn't be anything without him. His life became a map of what I refused to repeat, and everything I've built grew from choosing a better way forward.

I wasn't surprised by the estate he left behind or the debt tied to his name. He had lived messy and died messy, and the wake he left behind felt like an extension of everything that came before it. Most of the emotional work had been done years earlier—through boundaries, distance, therapy, medication, and the steady presence of the people who loved me well.

The reality of his death was more complicated. It stirred a mix of anger and sadness, along with the quiet disbelief that he had ended his life in such a stark, diminished way. My uncle had stopped by for a visit and was with him when he passed, just days after my father ignored the hospital's instructions—true to the pattern he lived by. As I tried to sort through the financial and logistical wreckage, a wave of anxiety hit hard enough that I asked my uncle to take over. The daily weight of his unfinished responsibilities was more than I could carry. What stayed with me most was the heartbreak of how it all ended: a man who once presented himself as polished spending his final years in a rundown trailer on the same property where the house had burned. The contrast was devastating.

The pressure of those COVID years had already pushed me to confront the patterns I had inherited. Learning to stay with myself during that season became the clearest line between the life I came from and the life I was choosing.

What remained afterward was a quieter understanding: I no longer had to leave myself behind to move through anything—childhood, crisis, grief, or the echoes of the past. Support, care, and honesty anchored me. And I let myself receive them.

Reframe Practice—You Don't Have to Carry It Alone

When pressure settles into your body, you might pause and

ask yourself one grounding question:
What support would help me feel steadier right now?

This practice is about noticing when your system is holding more than it needs to.
Support can take many forms—medication, rest, trusted people, or even a small shift that brings your breath back into your chest.

You may notice an instinct to manage everything on your own.
If so, you can gently offer yourself a different truth: *I am allowed to be supported.*

Let this become something you return to.
A quiet reminder that care is not something you earn by being strong.
It is something you deserve simply because you are human.

IV

Part Four

Before I ever found the steadiness I described in the years that followed—before the boundaries, the self-trust, the hard-won calm—there was the part of my life when the ground was first formed. The years when I stepped out of the world I was raised in and into one wide enough to change me. This next stretch of the story moves back in time, to the first miles of becoming myself.

10

The First Mile

There are moments in life when something shifts inside you before the world around you catches up. One of mine began on a winding road up a small Tennessee mountain, my car packed tight with boxes and bedding. My mother drove ahead as we made our way toward the college dorms where I would live for the next two years. I followed at a distance that felt steady and strange at the same time.

I was nineteen and trying to hold myself together. Leaving my hometown carried a sense of openness I had long wished for, yet it felt larger up close than it had in my imagination. As the trees closed around the road and the dorm buildings appeared through the branches, the reality of it pressed deeper into me. The separation, the shift, the start of a life beyond the one I had known—it all rose faster than I could manage.

Tears blurred my vision as I drove. I kept my pace behind my mother's car, wiping my face whenever her taillights came into view so she wouldn't worry. The tears came from the weight of entering a world where everything would be unfamiliar. My brother wasn't beside me, making jokes to steady my nerves. My mother was ahead, carrying her own mix of hope and heartache. And the road forward felt wide enough to steady and unsettle me in equal measure.

By the time we parked, I had tried to smooth my face back into a neutral expression, but the blotchiness gave me away immediately. My mother read it the moment I stepped out—she always has a way of seeing what I'm carrying.

She pulled me close, held me for a moment, and then helped me unload my things. We took boxes into a small room with white cinderblock walls and two twin beds, a room just for me.

For the first time, the space around me held no threat—only a quiet beginning.

I entered those years as a music major—classically trained, eager to learn, and unsure of how far my talent could take me. A full scholarship covered my tuition in exchange for performing, and music had always been the one place where my breath knew what to do. I joined the auditioned show choir, sang in the chapel, and studied under teachers who shaped me through structure rather than fear. They taught breath, discipline, and how to fill a room in a way that felt steady. I didn't know then how deeply those lessons would serve me later.

Performance class revealed everything. Each week, students walked to the front of a room full of peers and faculty, ready to offer something new. Nothing could be hidden. Every breath and every tremor could be heard. It was intense, but it gave me a sense of expression that wasn't tied to survival. My voice felt like an honest extension of myself. In one class, I finished singing "On My Own" from *Les Misérables* and burst into tears because not only did I feel the song's emotion, but I realized I was truly on my own for the first time in my entire life.

Some of the most lasting lessons came from outside the music building. One came from a psychology professor named Mr. Berger. His classroom was plain, but the way he spoke about the mind made it feel expansive. He taught us that people hold complexity, that a single moment never defines a person, and that dignity matters. His compassion for the topic shaped something in me long before I understood its importance. Years later, when he passed away, the news hit with the quiet force of losing someone who helped turn your life without ever knowing it.

During those same years, I met someone who would eventually become my husband. He first noticed me during a chapel performance, sunlight from the stained glass catching the edge of the stage. Later, he stepped into a conversation in the cafeteria with a line that made me look at him like he had lost his mind. My response—"Excuse me, do I know you?"—was sassy, but it didn't scare him off. He showed up at performances, brought me flowers, and once taped a note to my dorm window congratulating me on winning Miss Hiwassee before I even knew I had won. We spent evenings sitting outside the dorms, talking under the stars, sharing pieces of our lives that felt safe for the first time. Only later did I realize it echoed a wish I once made as a little girl under a Tennessee sky. Back then, I didn't know how much he would matter, but I recognized his steadiness from the start.

Those two years didn't give me all the answers, but they carried me forward. I learned how to stand by my choices. I learned how to reach for things because I wanted them, not because I needed to escape something else. I understood what support felt like, what belonging could look like, and how a life begins to take shape in small, steady movements.

I knew leaving home would change my life, but it opened it in a way I hadn't expected. Living on my own showed me that the years ahead could be shaped by my choices rather than by the history I came from.

Reframe Practice—Ask What You're Ready to Step Toward

When you're standing at the edge of a new beginning, you might pause and ask yourself:
What part of me is ready to grow now?

This practice gently shifts attention from fear to readiness.
Growth rarely arrives in dramatic leaps. Most beginnings take shape through one honest question and one small step.

You can let this question guide the next inch forward.

11

Becoming Someone I Could Trust

After breaking up with my boyfriend in 2004, Knoxville, Tennessee, became the first place where I felt space open around me—space I could shape rather than shield myself against. My days were long and often messy, stitched together by school, work, and emotions I barely had time to interpret. But Knoxville was also where I began to sense the faint outline of a life I could choose on purpose.

Working at the children's psychiatric facility was the first place where I understood what my voice could do. What started as a job to help pay the bills became a turning point in becoming myself. I remember walking up the steep hill and into the director's office, my hands shaking, unsure how my words would land. I explained that our kids needed more than structure and consequences—they needed skills, hope, and rhythm, something to anchor them to a future beyond our care. I asked for a budget, a raise, and a new position so I could build a life skills program.

He agreed. I walked out feeling taller, stunned, and exhilarated that the door had opened so fully. I'm pretty sure I danced out of the building.

The program became the heartbeat of our unit. We planted gardens and taught the kids how to replace overgrown weeds with something alive. I taught nutrition through games and activities so they could learn how to eat well on limited budgets. Every harvest we brought into the kitchen sparked a pride that softened even their hardest days. Those afternoons in the sun—hands in dirt, sweat on our foreheads—softened something in me, too. A part of me that had held tension for years began to settle.

My ambition eventually brought me to a hospital in Knoxville. I worked twelve-hour shifts in the emergency room, conducting behavioral health evaluations while finishing my bachelor's degree in psychology and managing a video store to cover bills. The ER stretched me. It asked for steadiness, compassion, and an internal rootedness I was still learning to build.

One evening, my director told me that every patient I admitted needed to carry a dual diagnosis—mental health and severe substance abuse—moving forward. Her expectation landed with a stillness in my chest. I asked clarifying questions, walked through our responsibility to the people in crisis, and listened as she stood firmly in her instruction. Adding diagnoses that didn't belong in a patient's chart would have carried consequences long after they left our care. Honesty had become a foundation in my life, and I wasn't willing to fracture it. I told her I couldn't align with that approach and understood if it meant I'd have to change my place there. She dismissed the concern and said she believed I would eventually adjust.

That night, I sat in my car absorbing the weight of the request. The truth was clear. When I returned for my next shift, I placed my two-week notice on her desk after she had left for the day. There was nothing left to negotiate. My decision held steady.

Leaving that job became the first time I chose to step toward myself rather than away from conflict.

Around that same time, I began a master's program in mental health counseling. For a while, it felt like direction, a grounded next step toward a career I respected. I loved the coursework, especially the way it connected human experience with possibility.

Group therapy was one of the required courses. We practiced in real time—sitting in circles, speaking our truths, allowing ourselves to be witnessed. My classmates opened themselves with a kind of ease that felt brave. When it was my turn, something inside me tightened. I felt the pull toward honesty, yet something in me guarded the stories I carried. I knew that opening them in that room would release more than the space could hold. So I listened deeply, supported where I could, and let the quiet reveal what I needed to understand about myself.

I recognized that the work of a licensed therapist required an emotional capacity I was still cultivating. I had spent years learning to carry my history with gentleness; taking on others' pain before I was ready could have reopened places I had worked hard to steady. I wanted my voice to support my becoming, not weigh me down.

One afternoon, while sitting beside a close friend during a lecture, a calm certainty rose inside me. I turned to her and whispered, "I'm going to the registrar's office after class." She blinked and reminded me I was only one semester away, but she could see the clarity on my face.

After class, I withdrew from the program and received a refund for the remainder of the semester. I drove to a Sonic, parked, and let the release come—relief, fear, and a sense of truth settling into place. When I called my mother, she listened and then exhaled with a gentleness that told me she understood. She said she felt relieved for me. In that moment, we both recognized what the decision reflected: I wasn't abandoning a dream. I was choosing a path that supported who I was becoming.

Around that same time, life brought someone back into my orbit in an unexpected way. A mutual friend from our college years had suddenly passed away, and Michael reached out on MySpace (remember MySpace?) to let me know about the memorial service in my hometown. I was already planning to visit my grandmother, so I decided to attend with a friend. I dressed a little nicer than usual, curious how he might react. He had only known me with blonde hair, and my natural dark-brown hair would be unexpected.

After the service, I saw him across the room and felt a warm recognition rise inside me. I walked toward him, and the moment unfolded with a familiar ease—steady, grounded, and filled with the comfort of shared history. We hugged, talked, laughed, and remembered our friend with the tenderness that loss often brings. The connection felt like rediscovering a part of myself I hadn't realized was waiting.

We stayed close after that day, letting conversations turn into connection and connection into something steady. From that moment forward, we began building the life we now share.

Through all of it—the facility, the hospital, the college years, the early leadership, the friendships, the heartbreaks, the love—I began forming a life rooted in steadiness. A life shaped by choice, truth, courage, and the belief that I could become someone I trusted. Someone who rose from authenticity, not performance.

Reframe Practice—One Small Shift

When you are stretching into a new version of your life, you might pause long enough to ask:
What's one slight shift I can make right now that supports who I'm becoming?

A shift might look like taking a steadier breath, choosing rest when you're worn out, telling a truth you've been avoiding, or loosening your grip on a thought that's outlived its purpose.

Small shifts shape whole seasons.

12

Quiet Foundations

Reconnecting with Michael marked a steady turning point in my adult life. We moved in together and began shaping a home built from our own decisions. We didn't have much money, worked long hours, and found joy in creating a life that felt like ours. It wasn't flawless, but it was real.

I often say I don't just love Michael—I genuinely like who he is. He understands the world I came from and responds to it with ease and kindness. He makes me laugh in the moments that need it most. He supports my mother and brother as though they were always his family, and he has never hesitated to fold them into our lives. He is my favorite person to navigate the world with, and I know how rare that kind of partnership is.

Our wedding was held on Saturday, September 26, 2009, a University of Tennessee football home game day, and it remains one of the brightest days of my life. Rain came down in sheets that morning while my mother and I set up tables under the pavilion beside the Tennessee River. By the time the ceremony began, the sky opened into sun and color—a rainbow stretching across the water, fireworks booming in the distance from the stadium—and it was the celebration that was perfectly us. A burrito bar, mini-cupcakes, music I mixed myself, and people we loved moving through the day without pretense. I smiled so much my cheeks hurt. Sixteen years later, the memory hasn't dimmed.

The morning after our wedding, we had brunch with our families and then drove our packed rental truck to Florida. We settled into a small house near Michael's parents, finding our footing as newlyweds in a place full of heat, palm trees, and vast stretches of sky. Michael encouraged me to take the first year off from work so I could have space to rest after years of motion and obligation. His insistence wasn't about tradition; it was about care. I will always hold that as one of the most generous choices he made for us in those early years.

During that time, I wandered into the local community theater. It became my first space in Florida that was solely mine. Rehearsals, backstage moments, and the fun of creating something with other people gave me room to breathe. I made friends who knew me as I was, not as I had learned to be. Show by show, my confidence returned in quiet ways.

Caregiving threaded naturally throughout our Florida years. Michael's grandparents lived close by, and Sunday visits became part of our rhythm. As their needs changed, we adjusted. We handled appointments, medications, and unexpected challenges, and spent slow afternoons listening to their stories. Their world shifted as they aged, and ours widened to meet their needs. Those years held a softness I still carry—time I'm grateful we had with them.

In 2011, my mother experienced a stroke shortly after moving in with us. Her speech was affected, so therapy sessions, doctor visits, and practice exercises at the kitchen table became part of our days. Her determination guided her recovery, and her progress showed up gradually—conversation by conversation, week by week. That season deepened the way our family moved around one another. Support became instinctive. Presence mattered more than anything.

Florida held nearly seven years of my life. Those years unfolded through routines, caregiving, work, and the shared effort of building a home. The responsibilities were familiar to me. I had carried roles like these long before, so daily life felt steady and lived-in rather than transformative. It was a season shaped by consistency, including appointments, theater rehearsals, shared meals, long shifts, and evenings spent catching our breath. The days felt complete and honest.

Those years also laid the foundation for our marriage. We carried the weight of responsibility together, learned each other's limits, celebrated small joys, and created patterns that still shape us. It wasn't a glamorous chapter, but it grounded us.

When Michael's grandfather passed away, the loss created a vacuum in our weeks. His grandmother had passed recently, and we had to adapt to yet another loss. Poolie, Michael's grandfather, was his first best friend, and his absence changed the air around us. Not long after, we talked openly about what we wanted for our future. We both felt the pull toward change—mountains, a cooler climate, more room to imagine the next part of our lives.

In 2016, an opportunity arrived that carried us to Colorado. We packed another rental truck, hugged his parents and Florida family goodbye, and drove west. Colorado waited—open, vast, unfamiliar, and full of possibility.

The foundation we built in Florida shaped what came next. The inheritance I received from my grandmother contributed to the down payment on our first home. Selling that home paved the way for our first house in Colorado. And selling that house made our current life in Parker possible. Each home carried a chapter of our story forward, built through work, partnership, and choices that created steadiness, one season at a time.

Today, my life looks nothing like the turmoil I came from. Michael and I built a quiet home in Parker—a place filled with calm, love, and the soft presence of our four cats—Schmidt, Cici, Jess, and Bootsie—who wander through our days like little reminders that gentleness can be a way of life. My mother and brother live with us too, all of us held inside this small fortress of peace and safety we've created together. It is a sanctuary, and we welcome only a few into it—those who value softness, respect, and quiet joy. I work from home now, serving people in a major healthcare organization, offering the kind of steadiness and compassion I once spent years trying to find. Our evenings and weekends are sacred and straightforward: games spread across the table, fireplace glowing, paint-by-number projects, shared silence in parallel play, a show humming in the background, kittens curled into the corners of the couch. It is an ordinary life by most standards, but to me, it is irreplaceable. It is peace at last.

13

The Long Way Forward

Every life follows a path. Some stretch forward in clean lines, smooth and predictable, with mile markers neatly spaced and the ground leveled by those who walked it before. And then there are the other paths, carved through underbrush, winding around fallen trees, marked only by footprints that survived the rain. These are the paths no one plans to take, the ones with uneven terrain and sudden turns, the ones that ask you to climb without knowing what the view will be when you reach the top.

My life has been the road shaped by necessity and choice, by instinct and hope, and a thousand moments that kept me walking even when I couldn't see what waited around the bend. For a long time, I believed the difficulty of the path meant something was wrong with me, that if I were easier, calmer, or less complicated, my road would have been, too.

I used to believe that a complex path demonstrated your worth. Now I know better. I know that it shows your experience.

When you plan an adventure, you pack what you think you'll need: maps, tools, warm clothes, water, provisions. But life never hands you a backpack at the trailhead. No one gives you a compass when you're born. You learn direction by getting lost. You know strength by climbing. You learn courage by falling and standing back up. You gather what you need along the way.

Looking back, I see the supplies I collected long before I understood their purpose—the intuition sharpened by reading dangerous rooms, the empathy born from loving people through their storms, the steadiness formed by holding others' emotions until they could hold them themselves. I didn't begin this path prepared. I learned through each step. I carried what I could. And somewhere along the journey, I discovered that the long way teaches what the shortcut never can: how to trust yourself enough to keep moving, even when the trail disappears beneath your feet.

And now, as I look forward, the trail still stretches far ahead. It rises and falls in ways I can't predict. The terrain remains uneven. The weather will shift without warning. There will be valleys that ask for patience and summits that ask for breath. There will be days when the wind nudges me forward and days when I'll have to lean in to it to take the next step.

But I no longer walk empty-handed. I walk equipped, supported, and aware.

Not because the road has smoothed, but because I am no longer afraid of the long way. It's where I found myself and learned to rise.

What I carry now isn't gear I packed intentionally. It's the kind of wisdom gathered through touch and tenderness, through grief and rebuilding, through loving and losing people I never wanted to live without. I carry the softness I learned from my mother, the loyalty I learned from my brother, and the patience I learned from my grandparents as their bodies slowed and their memories thinned. I carry the steadiness I learned from being Michael's partner—how love can be both anchor and wind, how two people can take turns being the strong one without keeping score. I carry the quiet pride of knowing I have been a place of peace for the people closest to me—not because I tried to be extraordinary, but because I showed up as myself.

Authenticity has cost me things. It has slowed me down in rooms where performance might have been rewarded. It has asked me to tell the truth when silence would have been easier. It has meant choosing integrity over acceptance, clarity over convenience. But the long way honors truth-tellers. And I would rather move slowly on solid ground than race quickly on a path that betrays who I am.

I've carried emotions that weren't mine to hold, too: the worry in my mother's voice, the anxiety in my brother's breath, the unspoken weight in the people I love. For years, I thought that was the only way to love someone:

lighten their load by taking some of it into my own body. I didn't realize I was doing it. It was instinct. It was muscle memory, a rhythm I had carried for years. I stepped forward quickly for the people I loved because that was how I had learned to care. And yet, in all those moments, I was shaping myself. I was learning the depth of my own capacity. I was learning where I end and where compassion can continue without consuming me.

I used to think maturity meant having everything figured out. Now I know it means allowing myself to learn.

I still apologize too quickly. I still brace before softening. I still overthink things no one else notices. But I also look at myself with more gentleness than ever before. Even the parts of me that feel unfinished are worthy of tenderness.

And maybe that's what the long way really teaches you—not how to rise flawlessly, but how to live truthfully. Not how to avoid struggle, but how to walk with yourself through it. Not how to erase your past, but how to honor it without letting it hold the map.

When I look ahead now, I see a horizon in place of what I used to see: a finish line. I feel deeper softness, steadier courage, and seasons when I'll carry others and seasons when I'll be held. The path is unmistakably mine because it's honest. Every step on it was taken by a woman who refused to disappear into the easier version of herself.

The long way I came was about transformation. It was about learning how to stay tender without breaking. How to be authentic without abandoning my truest self. How to love deeply without letting the past decide the shape of my future.

And now, with everything I've gathered, everything I've carried, everything I've healed, and everything I'm still healing, I feel a quiet truth settle into my bones:

The long way forward does not require me to be who I was.
It welcomes the version of me I'm stepping into next.
I don't know where the road leads next, but I know I'll meet it as myself.

And that feels like its own kind of arrival.

Reflection on Writing This Book

Writing *The Long Way I Came* wasn't about finally confronting a past I had avoided—I never avoided it. I had already moved forward, living my life with the lessons and strength it gave me. What this book allowed me to do was finally process it fully, give voice to experiences I had carried silently, and see them with clarity, honesty, and perspective.

Surprisingly quickly, the words came, as if the years of living and learning had been waiting to be translated onto the page. Each chapter became a milestone, each sentence a testament to growth and understanding. My father's passing gave me the space to do this work freely, without reservation, and with the emotional permission I hadn't allowed myself before.

This book is a tangible record of a journey deeply lived thus far—not merely survived. It is proof that we can fully move through our past, find meaning in it, and emerge stronger. I hope that readers will see not just my story, but the possibilities in their own, that complete processing, reflection, and growth are always within reach.

Remember your journey, because you have come so far. You are not alone. You are more than enough.

With my love and gratitude,
Andrea

About the Author

Andrea Haney Poole is a writer, leader, and lifelong observer of the inner world. *The Long Way I Came* is her first book—a reflective exploration of identity, resilience, and what it means to return to yourself after years of becoming what survival required.

With a background in psychology, business, and people development, Andrea has spent her career working at the intersection of humanity and systems. But her truest education came from lived experience—learning to listen to her body, protect what mattered, and choose alignment over approval.

She lives in Colorado with her husband, her family, and a house full of beloved cats, and believes that growth doesn't have to be loud to be transformative.